RICHARD NEUTRA

NEW ENGLAND INSTITUTE
OF TECHNOLOGY
LEARNING RESOURCES CENTER

DATE DUE

MAY 1 1990			
12·27·94			
JAN 2000			

38-297

THE MASTERS OF
WORLD ARCHITECTURE SERIES

UNDER THE GENERAL EDITORSHIP OF WILLIAM ALEX

ALVAR AALTO by Frederick Gutheim
LE CORBUSIER by Françoise Choay
ANTONIO GAUDÍ by George R. Collins
WALTER GROPIUS by James M. Fitch
ERIC MENDELSOHN by Wolf Von Eckardt
LUDWIG MIES VAN DER ROHE by Arthur Drexler
PIER LUIGI NERVI by Ada Louise Huxtable
RICHARD NEUTRA by Esther McCoy
OSCAR NIEMEYER by Stamo Papadaki
LOUIS SULLIVAN by Albert Bush-Brown
FRANK LLOYD WRIGHT by Vincent Scully, Jr.

richard neutra

by Esther McCoy

George Braziller, Inc.
NEW YORK, 1960

CONTENTS

RICHARD NEUTRA took up his career in architecture at a critical moment in the history of the modern movement. It was the place of his generation, he said, "to make true the promise of the grand revolution."[1] In the seventy years prior to 1920 —when his apprenticeship was well begun—the Iron Age had learned to span great spaces and had dabbled in prefabricated structural parts; the steel skeleton had replaced masonry in the Chicago of the eighties; reinforced concrete had been perfected as a self-supporting slab. Plate glass had ushered in transparency. The art of Japan, washing like a tidal wave over Europe and the United States, left in its wake an appreciation for lightness, elegance and a modular rhythm. Laws of physics were exploited to liberate structures from the earth: the old static equilibrium was replaced by a dynamic one.

The difference between Neutra's generation and the previous one was summed up by Eric Mendelsohn: "The Old gradually unclothes itself to nakedness, while the New is born naked."[2] Of the three men whose work meant a great deal to Neutra, two were born to the new style—Frank Lloyd Wright and Adolf Loos; while Otto Wagner, founder of modern architecture in Vienna, began in 1894 to strip away the plastic veils of the Renaissance. The First World War administered the *coup de grâce* to the handcraft movement, and the machine, no longer an evil spirit to be exorcised, was at the base of the new architecture. Neutra was one of the small group who accepted the discipline of the machine without coming under its tyranny. He saw the machine as an instrument that could create oases in the desert of mismade cities, houses relating to communities, and communities in the larger context of cities.

Although Neutra has designed for many countries and many climates, his architecture is an eternal search for the southland, cradle of civilization. Man "loves to immigrate to the south, or to conquer it," he wrote. "Like all Nordic barbarians we want to go to sunny Hellas, or to the land where the lemon blooms and no icy storms trouble us."[3]

Neutra is a modern classicist; his language, like that of the Periclean builders, is an artificial one, but both have used it to create harmony and beauty. His design has evolved slowly, and he has seldom strayed far from his original concept of architecture; in his early projects are the seeds of his later work. His project for an ideal metropolis, "Rush City Reformed," into which he deposited his ideas on design and city planning, was a treasure house from which he has drawn constantly throughout the years.

His philosophy of design grows out of his interest in the biological sciences, whose researches in man's responses to a multitude of stimuli furnish him a new basis for the understanding of the individual. Every aspect of building and every building material has been studied except human material, he says. "A workable understanding of how our psychosomatic organism ticks, information on sensory clues which wind its gorgeous clockwork or switch it this way or that, undoubtedly will someday belong in the designer's mental tool chest. Yet we must not indulge in mechanistic metaphors and thus oversimplify the issue of life, complex by the recurrent swelling of vitality and the ebbing into fatigue. Through more useful interpretations of our day, we have outgrown an adolescence that enjoyed itself in a gross machine materialism once considered 'so progressive.' "[4]

Richard Joseph Neutra was born in Vienna in 1892, the son of a mould-maker who became a joint owner of a small factory casting brass and bronze parts for the city of Vienna's gas and water meters. The boy first became aware of architecture through the subway stations designed by Otto Wagner (plate 1); he delighted in running up and down the wide steps with their low risers, and was enchanted with the unexpected view of the Danube caught through openings in the walls. The surprise of a fleeting view later became an element in his own architecture.

During his student days at the Technische Hochschule he was profoundly impressed by Wagner's break with masonry plasticity, the smooth covering used for the skeleton and the neatness of joinery. In 1910 he met Adolf Loos, "my master and fountain of ideas in architecture."[5] Loos, forty years old, had only then completed the first building which expressed his radical theories on the elimination of ornament—the Steiner house, Vienna (plate 2). Lack of clients had turned Loos into a polemicist. His whipping boy was the Secessionist group of Viennese designers who in the nineties had embraced Art Nouveau, a late European manifestation of Morris' English handcraft movement. Loos's faith was in an architecture whose forms grow out of the machine. His love for the United States—an unrequited one

—was based in part on our machine culture. Neutra called Loos "the most loyal American I ever met."

Loos, in a series of newspaper articles, praised the functional design of such American objects as spades and hammers, shoes and overalls; he called the oak toilet seat the most beautiful piece of cabinet work he had seen. But he had also discovered in America a new brand of humanism. "The story of Loos was in a way an immigrant's version of *Leaves of Grass*. Both were talking to me of men and women, only sketchily about the landscape or the height of buildings."[6] While still a student, Neutra spent several weeks in Loos's drafting room, working on a project for a department store.

Much of the important work done in Vienna during this time languished on drafting boards, and the modern architect was as famous for his projects as for his executed works. Revolutions made promises, as Neutra observed, but the fruits ripened slowly. The plans for Wagner's Vienna Museum, awarded first place in a competition, were executed first in mock-up on the actual site, and the feeling of the people of Vienna against a building of modern design next to their beloved Renaissance St. Charles Church was so bitter that the project was abandoned.

It was Loos's stories that first interested Neutra in America, but with the publication in 1911 of the Wasmuth portfolio of Frank Lloyd Wright's work, Neutra discovered "a fantastic living culture of some yet unknown people,"[7] and made up his mind to see it with his own eyes. He accepted at once Wright's cardinal truths— the open plan and the interpenetration of inner and outer space—while at the same time heeding Wagner's warning that modern architecture depended for its effect almost exclusively on simple forms and beautiful proportions.[8]

During the War Neutra spent three years as an artillery officer in the Balkans, returning to Vienna in 1917 to receive his degree *cum laude* from the Technische Hochschule. As Austria was then in a state of revolution, he went to Switzerland and worked in Stafa with a nurseryman and landscape gardener. Here his love of gardens was quickened, and under the tutelage of Gustav Ammann he learned to compose plants by their character and physiognomy to support a site creation. To Wagner's warning, Neutra now added another obligation: to cherish the site, and to give allegiance to the wider surrounding landscape.

In 1921 he was employed by the Luckenwalde Municipal Building Office in Brandenburg, Germany, which was resettling industrial workers from the city in semirural dwellings. "By living with my patients," Neutra said, "I took my own medicine." The relocated families, totally unprepared psychologically for country life, were a warning to him that resettlement is a risky act, unless the architect has an insight into the culture of the people to be rehoused. He had reason to recall Luckenwalde many times, once in Caracas while watching families from villages being marched into sixteen-story apartment buildings by well-meaning officials. Soon Neutra was put in charge of a project for a forest cemetery, with a chapel and gate house, his first executed design, except for a "water pavilion" in the Balkans.

In 1921 construction was started in Luckenwalde on a concrete and glass hat factory designed by Eric Mendelsohn. The expressionist sketches of the building so impressed Neutra that he went to Berlin to call on Mendelsohn. He found him making sketches of an addition to the *Berliner Tageblatt,* to the sound of Bach recordings. A few weeks later Neutra was installed in Mendelsohn's office as a draftsman and became, in a remarkably short time, a full-fledged collaborator. The addition to the Renaissance *Tageblatt* was a structure with long horizontal glazed bands; "its explosive, monumental, yet untraditional tower," Neutra said, "violated all municipal regulations." One of his duties was to intercede with the city building department.

In 1922, when conditions appeared to be more stable in postwar Germany, he married Dione Niedermann, a cellist, whom he had met in Zurich.

Although he spent close to a year and a half with Mendelsohn, Neutra carried away little trace of his expressionism. Circular forms emerging from long horizontal blocks, so characteristic of Mendelsohn, never entered Neutra's style. His use of the circular form is rare; his only buildings in which it is predominant are an auditorium for Orange Coast College (plates 144, 145) and the Lincoln Memorial Museum at Gettysburg (plate 120); in the ring-plan school project (plate 125), the buildings themselves are rectangular, as is the Von Sternberg house (plates 23–25), although the patio enclosure is elliptical.

One reason why he was more at home with geometrical forms was the conservatism of Vienna. The curved line was much in evidence during the "false Secession" (Wagner's characterization of the Secessionists) but by the time Neutra started his training, the straight line and the rectangle again reigned in Vienna. One must generally go to Neutra's plot plans and site plans for the curved line. He has always treated the building itself as separate from nature, and has held to the right angle, which is normal to his post-and-beam system; but nature does not know a straight line, and he has never imposed the right angle upon gardens.

In 1922 Neutra was in charge of the design of four Zehlendorf (Berlin) exhibition houses in which the living rooms were stages around which various rooms revolved. At the touch of a switch a study, a music room, or a dining room moved into position next to the living room. The closed-cube form of the houses, reminiscent of the postwar work of Rotterdam, had isolated windows, except for corner glazing.

Neutra had little opportunity to see the work of his contemporaries outside of Berlin, but ideas knew no national boundaries; and they were part of the air the architect breathed. By 1922, schools had already developed within the new style.

The organic school rallied around the work of Wright, and took heart from the architecture of Charles Rennie MacIntosh of Glasgow, and H. P. Berlage of Amsterdam; the rationalist school developed around the work and teachings of Adolf Loos, and the buildings of inspired engineers in iron, steel, and reinforced concrete. The rationalist school also owed a debt to Wright—the spiritual liberator of architecture—which Wright was prepared to acknowledge; he described the schools as branches from the left and from the right, "forced out from the parent trunk of an organic architecture."[9] Eric Mendelsohn spoke out against functionalism, calling it a transitional phase; ". . . function without sensibility remains mere construction," he wrote, and warned against "the falsification of the human spirit through mechanization."[10]

In 1923 Neutra collaborated with Mendelsohn on a competition for a business center in Haifa. The long, low buildings, unbroken by Mendelsohn's dynamic forms, appeared later in Neutra's work—as they did in future buildings of Mendelsohn's in Haifa. The business center, never executed, won first prize. Coincident with this was the crippling inflation in Germany, when prices sometimes rose one thousand per cent over night. This coming as a climax to the war and the rigors of the peace turned Neutra to the United States.

He found in the United States the conditions lacking in Europe that were favorable to the new architecture—our technology and our means of distribution. Sweet's Catalogue*—to him as exciting as a healthy forest to a Norwegian carpenter—was America's raw material.

His destination was Chicago. After a few months in New York, spent detailing Gothic ornament, he arrived on a rainy November day in 1923 at one of the forty-two railroad stations in Chicago and stepped out on what he called the door mat of the world. He arranged for lodging in Jane Addams' settlement house in the slums, then set out to find the broad acres in which he imagined Wright's prairie houses to be situated; he discovered them on city streets. He had looked forward "to facing the human beings who had been molded by the architecture of the future," but the original owners were gone.

Around him everywhere in Chicago was commercialized classicism, but still living there was Louis Sullivan, who had first treated the steel skeleton as material of architecture. Sullivan's accurate prediction that the Columbian Exposition would set architecture back fifty years had then twenty years to run. Neutra looked up Sullivan, and the young man told the dying one (Sullivan died in April, 1924) how his work had heartened the architects of Europe. There was a time, Sullivan admitted, when *he* had thought it would come to something.

At Sullivan's funeral Neutra met Wright—"It was like coming into the presence of a unicorn"—and when he visited Taliesin it was to him like going into "a

* A catalogue of construction, industrial and mechanical materials.

Japanese temple district." The following year he spent several months in Wright's drafting room. The only work on the board was a project called "Sugar Loaf," for a spiral-form motor hotel, which predicted the Guggenheim Museum.

Between his stays in Taliesin, Neutra worked almost a year as draftsman number 216 for Holabird and Roche; the office was designing "a box in a box, accommodated by one structural frame"—the 2400-room New Palmer House. This was Neutra's first opportunity to observe the organization of a big building, and he made running notes on every phase of the work during the months he spent detailing elevator shafts, and then as a liaison man between the architectural designer and all departments. His notes were woven into the book, *Wie Baut Amerika,* published by Hoffmann in Stuttgart, 1927. He tried to keep a picture of the finished building out of the book, for it revealed the depths to which architecture had fallen in Chicago since the nineties. Over the "quick" skeleton was a façade designed by a Beaux Arts architect imported from France; a Petit Trianon on the roof housed the mechanical equipment. The big offices had all become successful machines that by-passed architecture, although the drafting rooms were good training camps for design talent, Neutra observed. It was, however, this very decadence that made it possible for Neutra to establish a successful practice.

Neutra arrived in Los Angeles in 1925, and opened his own practice in the drafting room of R. M. Schindler, a fellow countryman who had been a student of Wagner's and had spent several years in Wright's office. Schindler had come to California in 1921 to supervise the construction of the Barnsdall house. One of the few projects on which they collaborated was a design for a competition for the Palace of the League of Nations, a nine-story building with an auditorium projecting over Lake Geneva; continuous glazing offered a view of Mont Blanc Glacier. As in all his early projects, Neutra introduced a heliport. The plan was one of three selected for a traveling exhibition arranged by the Deutscher Werkbund. The other two were by Hans Schmid of Basel and Le Corbusier.

Neutra's work falls loosely into two periods, the first spanning fifteen years, from the 1927 Jardinette Apartments to the 1942 Nesbitt house. The first period was one of exploration and discovery. His career had been delayed by the war and the paucity of building during the five years following the peace, and in California his creative energy burst out. His appetite for experimentation was ravenous; no one on the west coast, and few in America were so aware of the storehouse of materials and so excited by the possibilities of their use. He produced one after another a series of buildings that involved scores of new procedures and made imaginative use of new materials. But this was not industrial design, it was architecture. He

12

provided a basis, however, on which industry might have developed in harmony with architecture rather than isolated from it.

Neutra took nothing for granted in those early years of exploration, but re-examined every building practice; no member or detail or material escaped his scrutiny. His buildings of the twenties and early thirties brought into the folds of architecture various elements that would never again be alien.

His first work was in reinforced concrete, a material that had been used with considerable originality on the west coast.[11] In his 1927 Jardinette Apartments (plate 4) the long spans of the reinforced beams permitted large wall openings, which received strip windows; well-defined walls, with cantilevered balconies, alternated with glazed bands, in a smooth and precise composition. The skeletal structure was carried above the roof level, both for its sculptural effect and to disguise the "slums" which normally collected at that time on roof tops. In the manner of Le Corbusier, the marks of the form lumber were preserved on the exterior walls. It was the first building in the International Style in Los Angeles; an uncompromising and purposeful building, it owed little or nothing to Wright or to California. It predicted none of Neutra's relaxed—even lyrical—work of the fifties.

Neutra's developing style can be followed in three apartment houses executed between 1927 and 1942. The 1938 Strathmore Apartments (plates 5–8), shows a continuing interest in alternating bands of solids and transparents, in smooth surfaces, and in a modular rhythm. (The 3-foot, 3½-inch module, based on the width of the steel casements, was followed for some years.) However, the Strathmore's wood framing with stucco skin recognizes that a lighter material was suitable for California, and that it also constituted a great saving. The Jardinette has a lobby and long interior halls, while the apartments in the Strathmore are more like single dwellings with private entrances, which are turned toward an off-street hillside garden environment. By 1942, Neutra's floor plan was unusually relaxed, and although the exterior forms were still controlled by horizontals resting upon horizontals, the space within made greater demands upon the exterior. The Kelton Apartments, a transitional work, combined the reserve of the first style and the casualness of the later one.

The Lovell house (plates 13–18), whose plans are dated April, 1928, was Neutra's first large building after the Jardinette Apartments. It is often considered an isolated work, although it was part of an extended and patient exploration, and cannot be separated from the whole. It had in Los Angeles in 1929 an importance comparable to the early iron or steel and glass exhibition buildings in Europe, and indeed it was through this house that Los Angeles architecture first became widely known in Europe. Brilliant as the structure was in conception, it is doubtful whether it could have been executed without Neutra's familiarity with the methods of contractors and sub-contractors, acquired through his work with Holabird and Roche. He was quite aware that it was easier to be daring on paper than to deal with the building trades.

The open-web skeleton, in which standard triple steel casements were integrated, was fabricated in sections and transported by truck to the steep hillside site, and the lightweight bar joists of floors and ceilings were electrically welded in the shop. The shop work was held to a decimal tolerance to avoid the costliness of changes during assembly on the site, and as a result the skeleton was erected in forty hours —too fast to photograph the various stages of assembly.

The balconies, usually called cantilevered, are instead suspended by slender steel cables from the roof frame. This use of members in suspension, and also the U-shaped reinforced thin concrete cradle in which the pool was suspended, created a stir in architectural circles.

The walls of the house are of thin concrete, shot from two-hundred-foot-long hoses, against expanded metal, which was backed by insulation panels as forms. The rhythm of the transparent planes is broken by a two-story glass wall, opening a stairwell and one end of the living room to a view of a park, and the esthetic appeal of the house comes from these interpenetrating planes of glass and concrete walls. The plan, however, with its long interior halls on the upper floors, has little of the leniency achieved in his smaller houses of the same period. But none of the others has the ever-fresh surprise of the Lovell house—the Health House, as Neutra has always called it, because the client was a naturopath, and because of Neutra's beliefs concerning the relationship between health and architectural design.

After the Lovell house was finished Neutra was hailed as a technological wizard. Returning to Europe in 1930 as an American delegate to the CIAM conference in Brussels, he was invited to speak in Japan and at the Bauhaus. That same year, his second book, *Amerika,* was published by Schroll of Vienna, one of a series, "New Building in the World." In Holland he was handed a check by a Dutch industrialist, C. H. Van Der Leeuw, to continue his researches in another house. Upon his return to New York in 1931 he was asked to design a "Pullman of the Road" in aluminum for White Motors, and spent some weeks in Cleveland on the project.

The architect's own house (plates 21, 22) was built in 1933 from the Van Der Leeuw fund, and Neutra calls it the V. D. L. Research House. The lot, facing Silver Lake in Los Angeles, is only 60 by 70 feet; the house, designed to the setback lines, involved experiments on a modest budget. A standard wood frame is carried by precast, electrically vibrated concrete floor joists, which permit wide openings while avoiding the cost of steel framing. The main block of the house, two stories high, is joined by a hyphen to a one-story section, with a protected garden between. The decentralized plan has two living rooms and two kitchenettes, an arrangement admirably suited to a combined residence, in which three sons were growing up, and office, in which clients were received. Electrically operated sliding glass panels make the informal garden-living room part of the patio, and folding doors open the formal living room to a porch overlooking the lake.

An inspired detail developed here was the recessed light channel at the edge of the soffit, which illuminates gardens, takes the blackness from the glass at night, and at the same time acts as a curtain for the glass.

Neutra continued to use steel walls, prefabricated in sections, for the 1936 California Military Academy (plates 26–28), and again in 1937 for the Beckstrand house (plate 34). From industry he borrowed aluminum-coated steel in 1936 for the skin of the Von Sternberg house (plate 24), and devised hollow walls out of corrugated sheet metal flooring elements for the Beard house (plates 19, 20) in 1935. That his work had found popular acceptance is indicated by the Better Homes of America Gold Medal award for the Beard house. He tried out panels of diatomaceous earth* for floor and roof slabs in the Beckstrand house, and when cement and asbestos panels appeared on the market he used them for single-wall construction; in 1936 he designed an exhibition house of plywood (plates 33, 35). The panels are frankly expressed, and a neat detail was the aluminum molds at the joints of the panels.

The prefabricated house seemed to Neutra both sound and logical in America. Housing was the last of the industries to cling to handcraft methods, but the housing shortage, combined with organized mass production and distribution, made prefabrication seem to him an inevitability. His first effort in this field, in 1926, was an expandable house which he called "One Plus Two" (plate 29). Designed in pairs and sharing a wall, each had private outdoor living rooms. The diatom wall panels were suspended from cables attached to masts along the center line of the house; the prefabricated metal foundations could be adjusted to follow the changes of level of the site.

This house, and other schemes for prefabrication, remained projects or prototypes, but in them he developed ideas which became part of his design vocabulary. Indeed, all of his houses have been a search for the prototype, and while each has its separate identity it could serve as a basis for industrial production.

Neutra's preoccupation with technology cannot be understood out of context with the period between the two wars. During the depression years his interest was accelerated by the need for housing on the one hand, and on the other the widespread unemployment of men who could produce it. It was a time of the basic structure, basic English, and a struggle for basic sustenance. A picture of the period can be read in the plea made in 1932 by the Architectural League of New York to owners of vacant property to offer it for housing to the 2500 unemployed and

* Neutra saw in the abundant deposits of microscopic sea shells along the Pacific Coast a source material for lightweight panels.

destitute architects. A Wonder House exhibited in the same year in Wanamaker's department store in New York had hand-hewn shingles and manufactured worm holes in the floor planks; at the same time United States Steel called the prefabricated house as impractical as an all-rubber automobile; and also at the same time an appeal was made by individuals to the United States Shipping Board to turn a condemned liner into housing for evicted families.

The direct solutions that grew out of technology in the thirties are today called puritanism; but it was this high seriousness and dedication that doomed wonder houses and sheet metal gargoyles and Petit Trianons. Richard Neutra was one of that small band of men who turned the tide against such romanticism.

The architect is influenced by the materials he does not have, Neutra said, comparing Gaudí's Spain and Horta's Brussels. In 1942, with World War II three years old, there was little material of any kind available for civilian building; Neutra, making a virtue of necessity, designed a house of redwood board and batten, common brick, and glass. The Nesbitt house (plates 46–50) marks the beginning of a new period. He proved here that any material was the subject of his architecture. But the new style lay not in the new materials, which were themselves traditional, but in a new kind of transparency. In the Nesbitt house, the sliding glass doors of the entrance face a glazed wall, which give a "thoroughness" to the living area; this, and also the glass wall of the bedroom, predicated his later style more than the redwood. The surprise of the entrance, which appears more daringly open than it is, was an early attempt to break down the solidity of the front door. The plan itself created the privacy. In later houses he increased his attack upon the sanctity of the front door, until it lost all of its pomp.

Redwood remained one of Neutra's materials, although when used with stucco rather than as a continuous skin for the skeleton, it seems to be working against his design grain. One of his virtues has been in confining himself to few materials and exploiting them fully. Glass (the absence of material, the dematerialization of walls) has been his finest material, and the less emphasis given to the others that support the composition, the greater his success. Glass is the matrix of his design; as it became available in larger dimensions his design changed to receive it, and his plan increased in geniality.

The Kaufmann house, Palm Springs, 1946 (plates 51–55), moved in the direction of the pavilion, which is Neutra's last development in domestic architecture. Horizontal planes resting on horizontal planes hover over transparent walls. The material loses its importance—magnificent as the dry-joint stone walls are in themselves—and the gist of the house is the weightless space enclosed. The victory over the front door is almost complete; it is reached by slow stages, like the Mexican

16

house whose entrance on the street leads through a garden to an unemphasized door.

The house makes no attempt to re-enact the drama of the desert; it is linked to the desert only by boulders and planting native to the region. The house is not grown, it is constructed. Of this, Neutra was well aware. He wrote: "A dynamic plant that grows from roots which absorb moisture and nourishment from the soil is one thing; a static structural weight resting on waterproofed concrete footings is another."[12] A later instance in which the desert encroaches only in the form of rocks and planting is the Sorrells house, Shoshone, 1957 (plate 87).

The rectangle of the main block of the Kaufmann house loses its outline as the structure extends into the landscape: the louvred wall of the entrance walk terminating with the garage, the detached guest house on the north, and the continuation of a north wall to define a garden space, liberate the plan completely from the rectangle.

The Tremaine house, Santa Barbara, 1948 (plates 56–63), completed Neutra's search for the pavilion; the reinforced concrete skeleton is so effortless that the structure appears as a canopy over space. Columns placed at regular intervals support girders, and cantilevered beams carry the thin roof. The similarity to a Greek temple, open to all suns and winds, is inescapable. It is only at the entrance, where the roof floats over masonry walls, that the structure solidifies. But even here it dissolves in a band of clerestory windows, then reasserts itself in the strong columns which tie the thin roof to the ground. Clerestories are also used in spaces between beams in other walls, and have the effect of freeing the roof from the rest of the structure.

The site is a rolling meadow with fine live oaks and a view of woods and mountains, and the house is poetically placed under the oaks on a soft swell of land. The terrace off the living room continues in a long promenade raised on columns above the slope, and the space beneath is developed into a play area (plate 60).

A detail that Neutra was later to exploit fully is the butted glass at a corner of a room, under a wide overhang (plate 63). He used it with discrimination, always to draw into a room a distant view or intimate garden or, as in this case, the rough trunk of an oak. A late project in which it appears is the Düsseldorf Theatre (plate 173).

The cross-shape plan presses beyond its bounds in the form of a garden wall sheltering a dining terrace on the south. The one-room deep layout opens all the main rooms to the light and view on two sides.

By 1950 Neutra, uninvolved in complex structural problems and solutions, could settle down to the pure enjoyment of inner space. His simple and direct forms were unaffected by styles, and although he watched with interest Le Corbusier's excursion into plastic forms, and took note of the "new sensualism" in decoration and in ornamental engineering, his own post-and-beam work was aloof from the changing scene. A generation of new architects had grown up around him, some of them out of his office; three had found their own personal expression in architecture—Raphael Soriano in steel, Harwell Hamilton Harris in wood, and Gregory Ain in studs and stucco.

Only two new elements were noticeable in Neutra's work—water, and the outrigged structure. The reflecting properties of water were appreciated by Neutra in the thirties in the Von Sternberg house (plate 23), and structure was often extended beyond the roof line, as in Holiday House (plate 92). But by 1950 the reflecting pool and the extension of the structure into nature were constants.

The Moore house, Ojai, 1952 (plates 68–70), floats on water, and its hovering roof is repeated in wavering outline in the pool. In the hot, dry Ojai Valley, the water cools the air around the house, and the pool serves also as a storage well for irrigation purposes. By 1959 Neutra combined very effectively in many of his houses the reflecting pool and outriggers, i.e. posts supporting extended roof beams, sometimes called "spider legs." In the Moore house he had planted some of his posts in water, but in the 1959 Cole house, La Habra (plate 88), a series of outriggers crosses through the water and becomes delightful, integral decoration in the Japanese spirit. The two elements are combined again in the Singleton house, Los Angeles, 1960 (plates 89–91); here a single outrigger frames a distant view of the hills.

Outriggers are also used dramatically to support the swimming pool dressing rooms of the Brown house, Bel-Air, 1955 (plate 85). It is interesting to note here the clear definition of the walls and roof: walls read as walls, roof as roof, their identities are separate.

In the Lovell house, Neutra took some pleasure in calling attention to the changes of floor level behind the walls, following in the exterior the movement of the stairway from the third-floor entrance level to the ground floor. In the split-level Hansch house, Claremont, 1955 (plates 79–81), he opens to view and makes a design feature of the different levels of living room and bedroom wing.

His ability to wring every small advantage from the site is seen in the way structure is developed to accommodate distant views. Transparent walls open upon a panoramic view of mountains and valleys in the Moore house (plate 70) and the Kramer house (plate 74). His extensive use of butted glass under wide overhangs made it unnecessary to turn a house squarely to a view; he also opened up corners to bring a garden pool into a room (plate 73).

Twilight is a favorite time of day for Neutra, and the view from many of his living rooms is at its best in the evening; one can think that the living rooms are designed for homecomings, for certainly they perform brilliantly at night. Above all, his buildings have a high seriousness, and age does not detract from their dignity.

One of the astonishing things about Neutra is the way his thinking in house design is reflected in his public buildings, a reversal of what was once the typical procedure, the scaling down of the public building for the thousand-square-foot house. Neutra's solutions for the single house are the touchstone for such buildings as the San Bernardino Medical Center, 1955 (plates 99–101), built around a large court, with three patios cutting into the plan; the garden seen through glass is strikingly similar to the garden atmosphere of the entrance to the Kronish house of the same year (plate 78).

Holiday House, a seaside hotel at Malibu, 1948 (plates 92–96), has the same relaxation as the 1948 Bailey house (plate 64) built under the *Arts & Architecture* Magazine's Case Study House program. The material for both is redwood and glass. However, the aluminum and stainless steel of the Aloe Medical Supply Building (plate 111) of the same year is smooth and disciplined; there are many other such exceptions, but all of Neutra's commercial buildings have a human scale and a friendly noninstitutional atmosphere. The Northwestern Insurance Bulding of 1951 (plates 112–114) is as loose in plan as his houses of the same period. Halls and solid partitions are replaced by glass screens, and the main office is cross-lighted and ventilated. The building is just off Wilshire Boulevard, a street which grows more impersonal each year.

A delightful small building of Neutra's is the Gemological Institute. The very fine rear elevation demonstrates how Neutra can break up a cube form without being abstract. In the patio a most ingratiating spiral stairway to the second floor curves up over a reflecting pool (plate 118).

Beginning in 1949, Neutra was in partnership with Robert E. Alexander, architect and city planner, and out of their office came numerous schools and churches. The most striking of the churches is Miramar Chapel, La Jolla, 1957 (plate 123, 124), with its suspended stairway reflected in a pool, precast tree-form columns and warped roof. Designed by the partners and now under construction are the American Embassy for Karachi, Pakistan (plate 119), the Lincoln Memorial Museum at Gettysburg, Pennsylvania (plate 120), and the Hall of Records (plate 121) for the Los Angeles Civic Center. Associated with Neutra and Alexander on the Hall of Records were Honnold and Rex, James Friend and Herman C. Light and Associates.

SCHOOLS

Neutra's search for the land where the lemon blooms extended to the schools. His first essay in the open-air classroom was a project in 1928 for a ring-plan school. Individual detached classrooms were ranged around a large elliptical-shaped center field, and between the buildings were patios which were intended as instruction areas (plate 125). The plan was flexible enough to meet a variety of requirements, and the buildings, which would have lent themselves to prefabrication, could be constructed easily and economically. The creation of an off-street environment, both in the small patios and central gardens, and an assembly space, is a typical Neutra solution. One of the virtues of the elliptical plan is that it shortened the distance between classrooms.

The ring-plan school is presently being executed, after almost thirty years, in Lemoore, California. It was named the Richard J. Neutra School.

In 1926 most of the schools in Los Angeles were on small plots of land, were two or more stories high, with sanitary facilities in a basement, while long interior halls required daytime illumination. Classrooms had stationary seats, windows on one side only, and no access to playgrounds.[13] Neutra's ideas in school design grew out of the conviction that tensions begin to accumulate in a child when he is taken from the home and living room into a school and classroom, to be moored to the floor, and forced to look up at a teacher sitting above him on a platform. The vertical blackboard on the wall behind the teacher could also be disturbing to the child, because learning at home had taken place on the ground or on the floor, which were in intimate relationship to him.

Neutra saw great advantages in classrooms, especially for the elementary grades, which resembled living rooms filled with group action—but a living room such as only a handful of architects had conceived at that time, one connected to a patio by a movable glass front. He had a champion in Miss Nora Sterry, a teacher in the public schools who subscribed to John Dewey's theories on "learning through doing." But it was not until the earthquake of 1933, and the subsequent revision of the building and safety code governing school buildings, that Neutra's scheme was accepted. The safety factors involved in the one-story wood frame structure appealed more to the Board, however, than the daring plan. Because of its experimental nature the school was placed in an outlying district, on Corona Avenue in Bell, a decision the Board had reason to regret when the school immediately received national attention.

The Corona Avenue School (plate 126), set on extensive grounds, is one classroom deep, with communication between rooms by covered passages. (The indigenous Spanish Colonial architecture had made wide use of arcaded passages.) Practically all of the floor space is devoted to areas of instruction, a decided economy, and the rooms are bi-laterally lighted—on one side by a glass front and on another by high strip windows.

The Corona School banished the "listening classroom," which had its effect upon education methods, for the teacher became a part of the group as soon as

20

students were no longer restricted to fixed seats. A series of electrically operated steel-frame glass doors opens an entire wall to a partially paved terrace, and the students spill out from the roofed to the unroofed classroom.

In the 1936 California Military Academy Neutra worked in the same spirit as in the Corona Avenue School, although he used a prefabricated steel frame (plate 28). In the Emerson Junior High School, West Los Angeles, 1938, (plates 127, 128), a two-story building with an auditorium seating seven hundred students, he linked many of the first-floor classrooms to patios. By 1938 most of Neutra's ideas on schools began to pass into public domain. There is hardly a school built in Southern California today that does not make use of covered walks for halls.

A delightful interpretation of the open-air classroom is seen in the series of rural schools Neutra designed in 1944 for Puerto Rico (plate 129). The schools were part of a government program to raise health and educational standards on the island, and Neutra planned them as part of a village center which was composed of an assembly hall, health center and fountain, all grouped around a plaza. He saw these plazas as a nucleus for rural community life (plate 130). The schools were designed in units that could easily be duplicated by unskilled labor; each unit has two solid walls, a third with strip ventilating louvres near the ceiling, and the fourth with three wide glass panels that could be lifted like overhead garage doors to a horizontal position. During school hours the doors are always open. The school can be expanded easily by the addition of three walls and a roof. The rural health centers reflected local custom in the deep porches, which served as outdoor waiting rooms; an interior waiting room and milk dispensary had wide openings onto the porch. Neutra was granted a variance in the building code in order to ventilate the buildings by continuous louvres under the eaves. He demonstrated that the air flow under the eaves was more effective ventilation in a low-ceilinged room than the static air in a higher one. Urban schools, clinics and three district hospitals were also part of the extensive program. Little of the work followed Neutra's design except for the rural schools.

In the village-center scheme one comes close to the meaning of Neutra's planning. It has a relationship to his neighborhood squares—even the ring-plan school. The idea appears in still another way in a work in progress for Painted Desert, Arizona, where a school, visitors' center, and shops are grouped around a plaza. He likes the inward-turning plan—a deep memory in the human race, whether designed for defense, as in the clusters of stone nuraghi fortresses of Barumini, Sardinia, enclosing circular courtyards, or to achieve serenity for contemplation, as in the plan-around-a-quadrangle of the nunnery at Uxmal, Yucatan. Neutra looks upon the sheltered environment as a defense against mankind's modern enemy—progress.

Technology, which has benefited man, nevertheless "creates with each new invention urgent new demands on the human nervous equipment," Neutra says.

"It has become imperative that in designing our physical environment we should consciously raise the fundamental question of survival, in the broadest sense of this term. Any design that impairs and imposes excessive strain on the natural human equipment should be eliminated, or modified in accordance with the requirements of our nervous and, more generally, our total physiological functioning. This principle is our only operational criterion in judging design or any detail of man-made environment . . ."[14]

Schools have always been Neutra's great love, but it is typical of his habit of simplification that he should place them in a general category of buildings for "Humans in Groups." Among those not intended specifically for instruction is the Eagle Rock Playground Club House (plates 140–143)—a remarkable work, in which there is little distinction between art and life. Although Neutra achieved great sweeping spaces, by a system of lift-up walls, there is not a boastful line in the building. The east elevation (plate 141) has unusual clarity and directness; indeed the entire building is one of the fine understatements that Neutra so often permits himself in structure. He returned here to one of the devices he had used in the Lovell house by suspending the broad overhangs from steel cables attached to the roof beams. The main hall, planned for many uses, serves as gymnasium, dance floor, theatre and assembly hall, but the building is first of all a superb setting, not a utility structure. With the wide doors in the raised position the assembly room is little more than a covered space between stretches of landscaped grounds. The three-sided stage can face an audience seated in the hall, in a clubroom or in an amphitheatre.

Stages—in fact, every aspect of the theatre—stimulate Neutra to bravura; the revolving stage for the auditorium of Orange Coast College (plates 148, 149) can be used as a theatre in the round, and also can face audiences in two directions. In his project for the Düsseldorf Theatre (plate 174), the acoustics (Neutra calls it the auditive coloring) can be adjusted as easily as the lighting. "There is no reason why room acoustics should be static during drama, and only visual illumination dynamic," Neutra says.

In the Kester Avenue Elementary School (plates 136–139), 1951, the essentials of the open-air classroom were restated in a more refined form; in two Neutra and Alexander schools, the Alamitos Intermediate School of Garden Grove, 1957, and the Elementary Training School at the University of California at Los Angeles, 1958 (plate 146), the covered passages are light steel columns supporting steel flooring elements. Protected patios, large and small, continue in Neutra's ground plan for all the schools. Classrooms at the Elementary Training School are clustered around halls large enough for group activities.

Neutra's America lay half in his imagination in 1924. He saw cities as "profoundly in need of a methodology, of a rationale, of a systematic approach to wholesale planning and reconstruction."[15] Between 1923 and 1930 the solution that began to grow slowly in his mind was a project he called "Rush City Reformed," a layout for a model metropolis of one million population (plates 154–159). In the depressed-speed traffic lanes, which eliminate level crossings, below-ground-level parking and garages, and the parks separating speedways from multi-story apartment buildings, he anticipated the city plan of Brasilia, Brazil's new capital. (Twice during the building of this city he was invited to Brazil to speak.)

In Neutra's scheme the city block in the urbanized section was a long narrow strip, a shape which insured maximum exposure to the sun and eliminated inner courts. The ground floor of all buildings was open, and this wide space, as well as the streets, was given over to rolling traffic. The pedestrian walks, two and three stories above the street, were reached by elevators at street intersections, and shops were on the same levels as the elevated pedestrian walks.

The key to the layout of the city was movement. By treating the freeways, the local and express elevated train system, the railroad, the airport and docks as one subject, all forms of transportation were interlinked, and the city was kept fluid. An interesting feature was the landing strip for helicopters at the railway station and on the roofs of elevated stations.

But while charting the movement of the city he also planned for tranquility. He deals humanly with life in the neighborhood traffic-free plazas. These small man-scaled squares have always seemed to him of even greater importance than the extensive parks. In America he had missed the "face to face" squares, where one could pass an hour and be refreshed, and through his architecture he tried to re-capture them.

A variety of housing solutions was offered: eleven-story apartment buildings, prefabricated single transportable houses, one-story row houses, and grouped patio houses. He developed certain principles in Rush City Reformed that he was to follow later in his community housing. All houses, whether row, double or single, always faced onto green parkways, and children at play were thus safely separated from automobile traffic. The approach by automobile was through narrow streets at the rear of the houses. The second principle was to treat the property line as a legal fiction, in order to destroy the self-centered confinement of the individual house. Front lawns were common parks, not hedged or fenced-in, but shared. In all of Neutra's executed work his goal has been to enlarge the horizon and to ex-tend the property lines, as he says, to the stars.

His capacity to put his ideas to work in small projects while thinking in terms of cities is demonstrated in the Argent Place development on Silver Lake. In designing a number of individual houses for the street he developed a gracious interchange of grounds, while at the same time creating privacy.

In 1928 and 1929, when Neutra taught architecture at the Academy of Modern Art in Los Angeles, his students prepared under his direction numerous plans for the Rush City Reformed project. They included a prison with school, built around a large open court, and a beach development. For the latter he designed an open-angled, multiple-story hotel, vacation cottages and extensive recreational areas near the water. Among his students were many who were dissatisfied with their training in schools of architecture, which in 1928 acknowledged none of the new trends in design. Since that time Neutra has continued his apprenticeship program in his office.

A project for a community of six hundred families in Jacksonville, Florida, 1939, has a boot-shaped ground plan, with through traffic at the perimeter; double rows of houses facing parks grow in fingerlike forms from the freeways inward, pointing toward a great central park that stretches the length of the plan (plate 160). The merging of the finger parks into the greater open green is a rich and beautiful use of land which could serve as a model for developments today.

In the Amity project for Compton, 1939 (plates 162, 163), a mutual-ownership development administered by the Federal Works Agency, and in Hacienda Village, 1941, East Los Angeles, a development for Negroes and Mexicans, the finger park scheme was again used.

The two plans for National Youth Administration Center, designed in 1939, when Neutra was a member and later chairman of the California State Planning Board, are impressive for the freedom of the ground plan and the architectural considerations brought to buildings (plate 161) which might have turned out to be barracks. He achieved real distinction by turning and twisting the plan to embrace courts and gardens, and by joining the groups of buildings by covered walks. Through the ground plan he accorded dignity to the individual, even when the budget and common practice suggested a rigid interpretation.

In 1942, Neutra's gifts as a site planner and architect were at last given a worthy outlet. He was commissioned by the Federal Public Housing Authority to design 600 dwellings for a rolling site cut by canyons. In Channel Heights (plates 164–169), a housing development for wartime shipyard employees and their families in San Pedro, he found his way through bureaucratic complexities to express fully his ideals.

The plan drew much of its importance from the subtle use of what was considered an unfortunate site. Instead of going in with bulldozers and leveling, he fitted the houses to the contours of the land. The land was treated as a park, and the one- and two-story houses were subtly integrated in articulated groups in the

24

landscape. It was perhaps the only war housing development that was not handled as a drawing board problem. It remained as permanent housing for many years because of the friendliness of gardens around the houses, and the ocean view to which the houses were all opened. A community was created, one which included schools, nurseries, community hall, health center, shops—even a garden work center, where the rudiments of gardening could be learned. Neutra designed economical, lightweight furniture for the houses, which helped to maintain an openness in the living room (plate 169).

In the fifties Neutra and Alexander collaborated on a ten-year master plan for the Island and the free port of Guam, and on a number of urban redevelopment plans, one for the urbanized area of Sacramento and a later one for Tulsa. The Sacramento plan developed an interflow between a low-lying blighted district and the present business center, built on a higher level, a scheme which gave the city an opportunity to reclaim the blighted area and put it to use as parking space, while expanding the upper level in multiple-story buildings. Another project was Elysian Park Heights, a planned community for 3400 families on a 160-acre piece of land cut up by canyons (plate 172). An ideal location, it adjoined the little-used Elysian Park, and skirted two new freeways. The land was ten minutes from Los Angeles City Hall. With the population of Los Angeles increasing at the rate of one thousand each month, the new community would have eliminated a great deal of senseless commuting. Wide-spaced multi-story apartment houses were planned to house most of the families, with numerous one-story row and single dwellings placed on the alluvial fill unsuitable for larger buildings. The planned density was twenty-one families per acre. After the working drawings were entirely completed, the City Housing Authority canceled the project. It was an inestimable loss to Los Angeles, so desperately in need of good planning, especially for low-income families. In the meantime, Los Angeles continues to sprawl individualistically, swallowing up possible park sites, uprooting trees, bulldozing away the natural contours of the land to produce the self-centered sixty-foot front lot. Neutra's concern over such problems is voiced in his book, *Survival Through Design*.

"The common use space for the community gathering area of our towns has shrunk disastrously, although pavement may amount to as much as a deplorable 35 per cent of the total urban ground." Crowded as the medieval cities were, he noted, "they had both a cultural focus as well as a 'nature reserve' just beyond the city gates a few hundred steps off. Attic windows of their houses—and minds as well—could look over the city walls into a landscape of natural functioning."[16]

Neutra has played a role in bringing his own city into cultural focus, and not a little of this has been accomplished by bringing technique into focus with architecture. In approaching design without illusions and prejudices he established new esthetic standards, ones which transcend style or forms. During the decade in which

25

his firm was Neutra and Alexander, his forms were more venturesome: the undulating roof of the Embassy; the plastic character of the columns of the La Jolla Chapel; the dramatic tensions external to the skeletal frame of the Ferro Chemical Building (plate 122). But his essential boldness does not lie in forms created but in correct and imaginative procedure; as a result, his forms have a universality. They also embrace what he called "the beauty of the small," learned while in Japan in 1930.

"Imagination and science—what more has any great work of art ever required?"[17]

NOTES

1. *L'Architecture d'Aujourd'hui,* June, 1948, p. 6.

2. *Architectural Record,* December, 1927.

3. Neutra, unpublished autobiography.

4. Neutra, *Survival Through Design,* Oxford University Press, New York, 1954, p. 191.

5. Neutra, unpublished autobiography.

6. *Ibid.*

7. *Ibid.*

8. *Otto Wagner,* Vol. III, Books V, VI, VII, Holzhausen, Vienna, 1904, p. 9.

9. "What the Cause of Architecture Needs Most, Frank Lloyd Wright," *Architectural Review,* March, 1937, p. 99.

10. Arnold Whittick, *Eric Mendelsohn,* Faber and Faber, London, 1940, p. 75.

11. In Los Angeles in 1912, a former Sullivan draftsman, Irving Gill, moving in the same direction but independently of Adolf Loos, perfected a slab-tilt system in which steel window and door frames were integrated in a reinforced concrete slab; in 1914 he lifted walls 60 feet long for the La Jolla Community Center. R. M. Schindler devised a slab-tilt system for four-foot tapered concrete walls for his 1921 office and residence in Los Angeles; in 1923 he used lift-form for an apartment court in La Jolla, and in his 1926 Lovell beach house he hung prefabricated walls from a series of pre-cast concrete frames. Lloyd Wright made use of lift-form for a 1915 hotel in Riverside, and tried out textured concrete blocks in 1919.

12. Neutra, *Survival Through Design,* p. 89.

13. One of the precedents for the school was Bruno Taut's 1927 Municipal School at Berlin-*Neükoln,* in which folding doors open an entire wall of a classroom to a terrace, protected by a wide overhang; the room is lighted by clerestories on three sides. See *Modern Architecture,* Bruno Taut, A. and C. Boni, New York, 1929, p. 173; also *Terrassen Typ,* Richard Döcker, Wedekind, Stuttgart, 1929, pp. 88, 89. A second precedent was Irving Gill's 1931 kindergarten in Oceanside, in which classrooms are staggered, and French doors filling a 16-foot opening, protected by overhangs, are oriented to play yards. See *Catalogue: Irving Gill Exhibition* by this writer, Los Angeles County Museum, 1958, p. 59.

14. *Survival Through Design,* p. 86.

15. Unpublished autobiography.

16. *Survival Through Design,* p. 350.

17. Herbert Read, *Art and Industry,* Horizon Press, New York, 1954, p. xv.

SELECTED BIBLIOGRAPHY OF BOOKS AND ARTICLES WRITTEN BY RICHARD NEUTRA

BOOKS

Wie Baut Amerika, Hoffman-Verlag, Stuttgart, 1927.
Neues Bauen in der Welt: Amerika, Verlag Anton Schroll, Vienna, 1930.
Architecture of Social Concern, Gerth Todtman, São Paulo, Brazil, 1948.
Mystery and Realities of the Site, Morgan & Morgan, New York, 1951.
Survival Through Design, Oxford University Press, New York, 1954.
Life and Human Habitat, Alexander Koch, Stuttgart, 1956.
Realismo Biologico, Jorge Grisetty, Buenos Aires, 1958.
Autobiography, in preparation.

ARTICLES

"New Architecture has a Pedigree," *T-Square,* January, 1932.
"New Building in Japan," *Shelter,* November, 1932.
"New Elementary Schools for America," *Architectural Forum,* January, 1935.
"Governmental Architecture in California," *Arts & Architecture,* August, 1941.
"Diatalum Dwellings," *Architectural Forum,* September, 1942.
"Peace Can Gain From War's Forced Changes," *New Pencil Points,* November, 1942.
"Los Angeles Inventory—Housing, a Definition," *Arts & Architecture,* January, 1943.
"Observations on Latin America," *Progressive Architecture,* May, 1946.
"Sea-Land Transfer," *Architectural Record,* September, 1946.
"Prefabrication from Survival Through Design," *Arts & Architecture,* June, 1950.
"American Architecture in a Lifetime," *Architectural Design,* England, August, 1951.
"Housing in Mild Climates," *Progressive Architecture,* October, 1953.
"Philosophy of Structures," *Student Publication, School of Design,* North Carolina State College, October, 1954.
"Building Before Drawing," *Journal of the American Institute of Architects,* April, 1955.
"The Patio House," *House and Home,* August, 1956.
"Urban Design," lecture, Urban Design Conference, Harvard College, Spring, 1956, published in *Progessive Architecture,* September, 1956.
"Life's Human Defenses," *Frontier* (Los Angeles), February, 1957.
"Shapes on a Campus Are not Extracurricular," lecture, Conference on Higher Education, Chicago, March, 1957.

SELECTED BIBLIOGRAPHY ON
RICHARD NEUTRA

BOOKS

Bruno Zevi, *Richard Neutra,* Il Balcone, Milan, Italy, 1954.

W. Boesiger, ed., *Richard Neutra, Buildings and Projects,* Editions Girsberger, Zürich, 1951 (contains complete bibliography).

W. Boesiger, ed., *Richard Neutra, Buildings and Projects 1950-1960,* Editions Girsberger, Zürich, 1959 (contains complete bibliography).

ARTICLES

"The Garden Apartment House," *Christian Science Monitor,* July 12, 1928.

"Stores the Road Passes Through," *Nation's Business,* July, 1929.

"Little Red School House, What Now?" *Fortune,* February, 1935.

"Studies in Recent Prefabrications," *American Architect and Architecture,* September, 1936.

"Richard J. Neutra, A Center of Architectural Stimulation," *Pencil Points,* July, 1937.

"The Architecture of Richard J. Neutra," *Shelter,* March, 1938.

"Richard J. Neutra, Architect," *Housing,* September, 1941.

"Three Privately Developed Apartment Houses," *Pencil Points,* January, 1944.

Time, February 2, 1947.

L'Architecture d'Aujourd'hui, June, 1948. Neutra issue, with two special articles, "A Visit to Neutra," by Marcel Lods, and "A Twentieth Century Architect," by Alexandre Persitz.

Newsweek, May 28, 1951.

"Neutra, Contemporary Classicist," *Fortnight,* September 17, 1951.

"Richard Neutra," monograph in *Kokusai Kenchiku,* Tokyo, Japan, 1952.

"Roots of California Contemporary Architecture," Catalogue for Exhibition, sponsored by Municipal Art Department and Architectural Panel, Los Angeles, 1956. Text by Esther McCoy.

"Richard Neutra," monograph by Frederick Wight for Neutra exhibition at the University of California at Los Angeles, 1959.

"Profile: Richard J. Neutra," *Pacific Architect and Builder,* May, 1960.

SOURCES OF ILLUSTRATIONS

Almost all the photographs reproduced in the following pages were made by the photographer JULIUS SHULMAN of Los Angeles.

Exceptions include plates 1-3, courtesy of the author; plate 4 (Luckhaus Studio, Los Angeles) and all drawings and sketches, courtesy of the office of Richard Neutra.

1. Otto Wagner, Karlsplatz Subway Entrance, Vienna, 1894.

2. Adolf Loos, Steiner House, Vienna, 1910.

3. Painting of Los Angeles in the 1850's.

5. Strathmore Apartments, Los Angeles, 1938.

6. Strathmore Apartments. Plan.

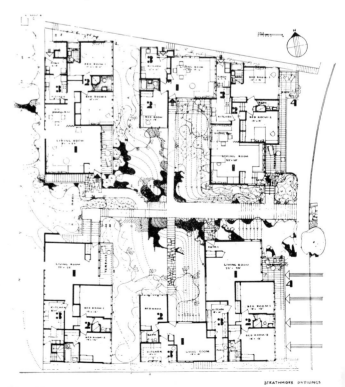

4. Jardinette Apartments, Los Angeles, 1927.

7. Strathmore Apartments. East view.

8. Strathmore Apartments.

9. Kleveman Apartments. Sketches.

10. Kleveman Apartments, Los Angeles, 1948. Exterior detail.

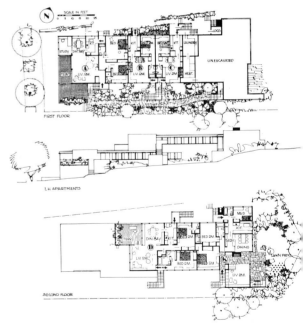

11. Kleveman Apartments. Plans, elevation.

12. Landfair Apartments, Los Angeles, 1938. Northwest view.

13. Lovell (Health) House, Los Angeles, 1929.

14. Lovell House. Steel frame.

15. Lovell House. General view.

16. Lovell House. Site plan.

17. Lovell House. Living room.

18. Lovell House. Living room.

19. Beard House, Altadena, 1935.

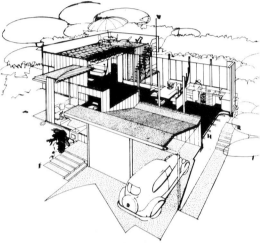

21. Neutra House, Los Angeles, 1933.

20. Beard House. Perspective sketch.

22. Neutra House. View of garden room from patio.

23. Von Sternberg House, Los Angeles, 1936. Entrance.

24. Von Sternberg House.

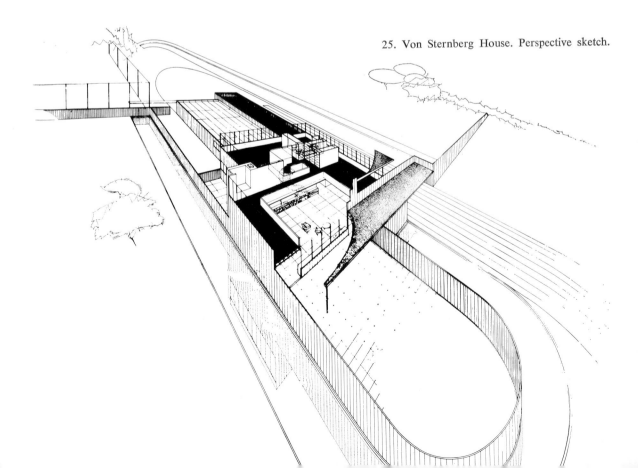

25. Von Sternberg House. Perspective sketch.

26. California Military Academy, West Los Angeles, 1936. Classroom wing.

27. California Military Academy. Erection of prefabricated steel elements.

28. California Military Academy. Prefabricated window walls.

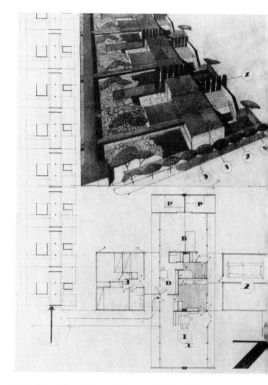

29. One Plus Two Houses (Rush City Reformed), 1926 (Project).

30. Multistory Parking Garage, 1940 (Project).

31. Universal Pictures Building,
Los Angeles. 1930. Cafe entrance.

32. Catalina Ticket Office, Los Angeles, 1933. Interior.

33. Plywood Model House, 1936. View from garden.

34. Beckstrand House, Palos Verdes, 1937. View from west.

35. Plywood Model House, 1936.

36. Diatom Prefabricated House, 1923.

37. J. N. Brown House, Fishers Island, New York, 1936. Exterior detail from east.

38. J. N. Brown House. View toward bay and ocean.

39. J. N. Brown House. Perspective sketch.

40. Berger House, Hollywood, 1939. View from south.

41. McIntosh House, Los Angeles, 1937.

42. McIntosh House. Exterior detail.

43. Kahn House, San Francisco, 1940.

44. Kahn House. Furniture designed by Richard Neutra.

45. Kahn House. Furniture designed by Richard Neutra.

46. Nesbitt House, West Los Angeles, 1942. Entrance.

47. Nesbitt House. Entrance Hall.

48. Nesbitt House. Bedroom

49. Nesbitt House. Entrance court.

50. Nesbitt House. Plan.

SCALE IN FEET
0 5 10 15 20 25

51. Kaufmann (Desert) House, Palm Springs, 1946. View toward south.

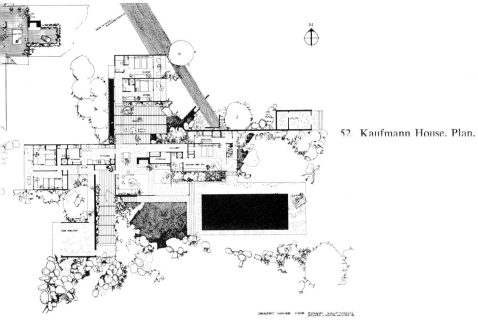

52. Kaufmann House. Plan.

DESERT HOUSE FOR EDGAR KAUFMANN
RICHARD J. NEUTRA ARCHITECT

53. Kaufmann House. Exterior detail.

54. Kaufmann House. Exterior detail.

55. Kaufmann House. Roof porch.

56. Tremaine House, Santa Barbara, 1948. Living room seen from exterior.

57. Tremaine House.

58. Tremaine House. Entrance.

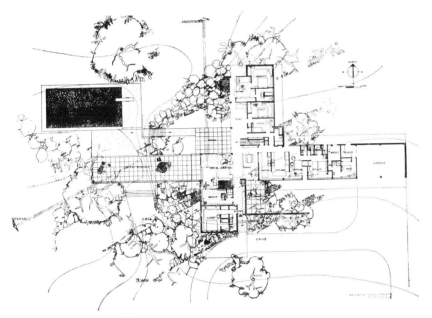

59. Tremaine House. Plan.

60. Tremaine House. View from roof, raised terrace at left.

61. Tremaine House. View of living room.

62. Tremaine House. View of living room toward library.

63. Tremaine House. View of bedroom wing.

64. Bailey House (*Arts and Architecture* Case Study House), 1946.

65. Hinds House, Los Angeles, 1951.

66. Hinds House. Bedroom.

67. Hinds House. Plan.

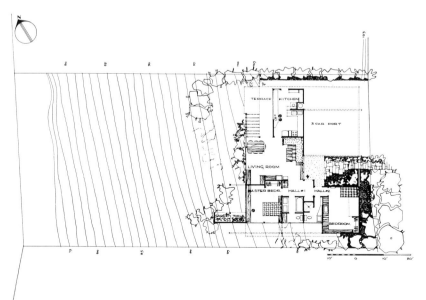

68. Moore House, Ojai, 1952.

70. Moore House. View toward north.

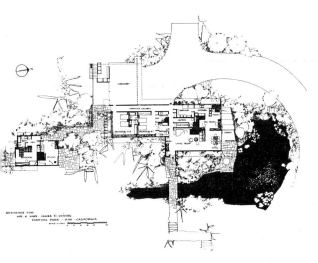

69. Moore House. Plan.

72. Dining chairs and "camel" table by Richard Neutra.

73. Goodman House, San Bernadino, 1952.

74. Kramer House, Corona, 1953. View from living room.

75. Kronish House, Beverly Hills, 1955. Entrance.

76. Kronish House.

77. Kronish House. Living room terrace.

78. Kronish House. Entrance from interior.

80. Hansch House. View from south.

79. Hansch House. Living room and bedroom levels.

81. Hansch House, Claremont, 1955.

82. Serulnic House, Tujunga, 1955. Living room.

83. Hammerman House, Los Angeles, 1956. Kitchen.

84. Brown House, Bel-Air, 1955.
Bedroom wing over garage.

85. Brown House. Bathhouse near pool.

86. Brown House. Living room.

87. Sorrells House, Shoshone, 1957. Terrace.

88. Cole House, La Habra, 1959. Patio.

89. Singleton House, Los Angeles, 1959. View from living room.

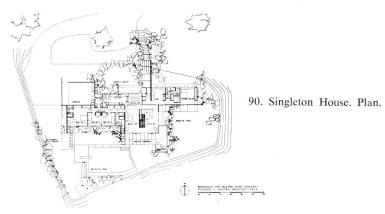

90. Singleton House. Plan.

91. Singleton House. View from south.

92. Holiday House, Malibu, 1948.

93. Holiday House. Exterior detail of corner apartment.

94. Holiday House. Lobby interior.

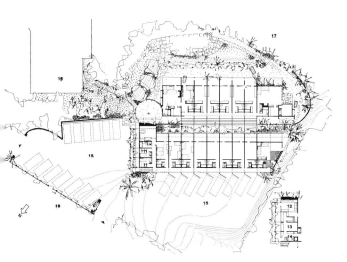

95. Holiday House. Plan.

96. Holiday House. Court between apartment units.

97. San Pedro Community Hotel, Los Angeles, 1953 (Neutra and Alexander).

98. San Pedro Community Hotel. Dining room.

99. San Bernardino Medical Center, San Bernardino, 1955.

100. San Bernardino Medical Center. Patio.

101. San Bernardino Medical Center. Waiting room for pediatrician.

102. Planetarium, Los Angeles, 1931.

103. Dayton Museum. Sketch showing planetarium.

104. Dayton Museum, Dayton Ohio, 1956 (Neutra and Alexander).

105. Child Guidance Clinic (University of Southern California) Los Angeles, 1960.

106. National Charity League, Los Angeles, 1960. Exterior detail.

107. National Charity League.

108. National Charity League. Patio.

109. National Charity League. Playground.

110. Aloe Medical Supply Building, Los Angeles, 1948. "Cantilever light."

111. Aloe Medical Supply Building. Façade detail.

112. Northwestern Insurance Building. Exterior detail.

113. Northwestern Insurance Building, Los Angeles, 1951.

114. Northwestern Insurance Building, Entrance.

115. Amalgamated Clothing Workers of America Building, Los Angeles, 1957, (Neutra and Alexander).

116. Amalgamated Clothing Workers of America Building. Ceiling detail.

117. Logar Store, Granada Hills, 1955 (Neutra and Alexander).

118. Gemological Institute, Los Angeles, 1956. Spiral staircase in patio.

119. American Embassy, Karachi, Pakistan, (Project, Neutra and Alexander). Model.

120. Lincoln Memorial Museum, Gettysburg, Pennsylvania (under construction) (Neutra and Alexander). Perspective sketch.

121. Hall of Records, Los Angeles, 1958 (Neutra and Alexander). Perspective sketch.

122. Ferro Chemical Company, Cleveland, Ohio, 1957 (Neutra and Alexander).

124. Miramar Chapel, Interior.

3. Miramar Chapel, La Jolla, 1957 (Neutra and Alexander). Suspended stairway (opposite page).

125. Ring Plan School, 1928. (Project.) (Now under construction as Richard J. Neutra School, Lemoore.)

126. Corona Avenue School, Los Angeles, 1935.

127. Emerson Junior High School, West Los Angeles, 1938.

127a. Emerson Junior High School. Overall view, auditorium at left.

128. Emerson Junior High School. Steel skeleton.

129. Scheme for Rural Schools, Puerto Rico, 1944. Typical classroom.

130. Scheme for Rural Community Centers, Puerto Rico, 1944.

131. Caguas District Hospital, Puerto Rico, 1944 (Project, Neutra and Alexander).

132. Adelup School, Oceania, Guam, 1951 (Neutra and Alexander). View from north.

133. Adelup School.

134. Governor's House, Guam, 1952 (Neutra and Alexander).

135. Sanatorio Universitario
Italiano, 1948-50 (Project).
Plan.

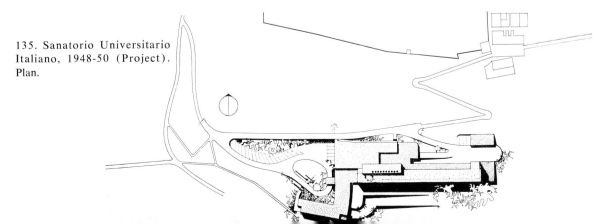

136. Kester Avenue Elementary School, Los Angeles, 1951. Perspective sketch.

137. Kester Avenue Elementary School, View from east.

138. Kester Avenue Elementary School. Patio play-yard.

139. Kester Avenue Elementary School. Play area.

140. Eagle Rock Club House. View along east front.

141. Eagle Rock Club House, Los Angeles, 1953.

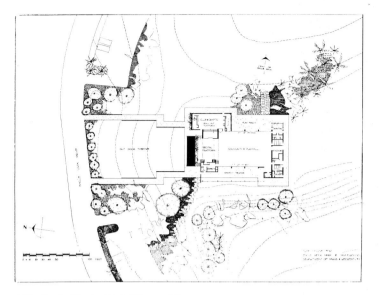

142. Eagle Rock Club House. Plan.

143. Eagle Rock Club House. View across stage toward outdoor theater.

144. Orange Coast College, Costa Mesa, 1957 (Neutra and Alexander).

145. Orange Coast College. Auditorium concourse.

146. Elementary Training School, University of California, Los Angeles, 1958 (Neutra and Alexander). Patio between classrooms.

147. Orange Coast College. Concourse detail.

148. Orange Coast College. Auditorium interior.

149. Orange Coast College. Stage detail.

150. St. John's College, Annapolis, Maryland, 1958 (Neutra and Alexander). Auditorium interior.

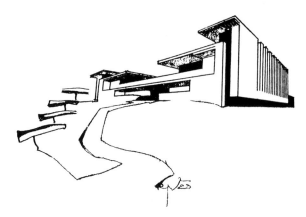

151. University Library for Near East, 1923 (Project).

152. San Fernando State College Fine Arts Building. Detail of façade louvers.

153. San Fernando State College Fine Arts Building. San Fernando, 1959.

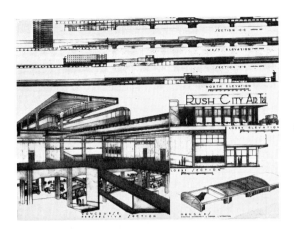

154. Rush City Reformed, 1923-30 (Project). Air terminal sketches.

155. Rush City Reformed. Inner city blocks.

156. Rush City Reformed. Business center, all cross traffic eliminated.

157. Rush City Reformed. Reinforced concrete store and office building.

158. Rush City Reformed. Row houses with community center.

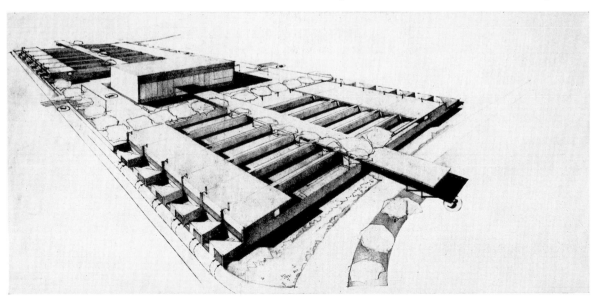

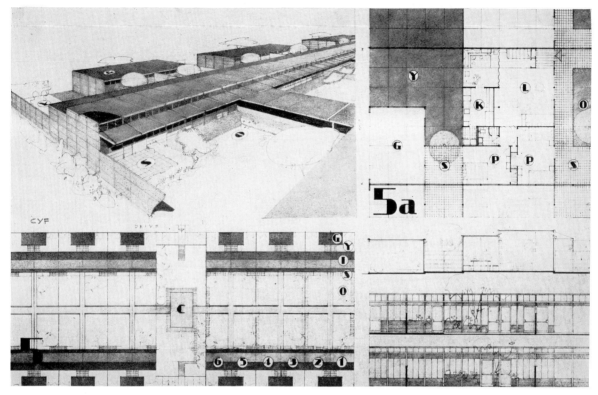

159. Rush City Reformed. Patio housing.

160. Park Living Colony, Jacksonville, Florida, 1939 (Project). Site plan.

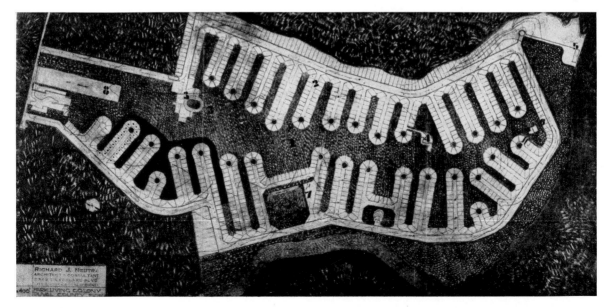

161. National Youth Administration Center, San Luis Obispo, 1939.

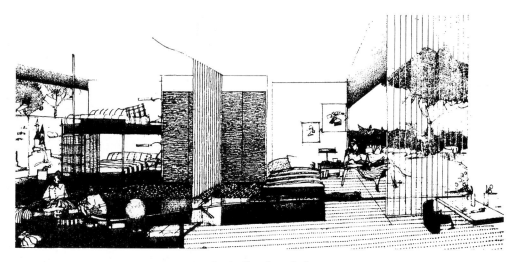

162. Amity Village, Compton, 1943 (Project). Sketch, twin houses.

163. Amity Village. Village house interior.

164. Channel Heights Housing, San Pedro, 1943.

165. Channel Heights Housing.

166. Channel Heights Housing. Site model.

167. Channel Heights Housing. Houses facing commons.

168. Channel Heights Housing. Shopping center, manager's office monitor booth.

169. Channel Heights Housing. Interior, single apartments.

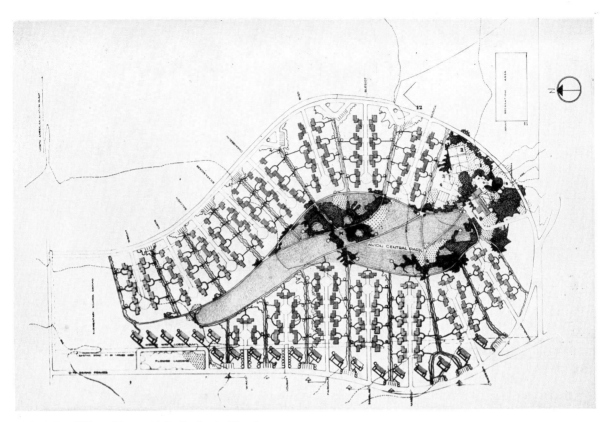

170. Avion Village, Texas, 1942 (Project). Site plan.

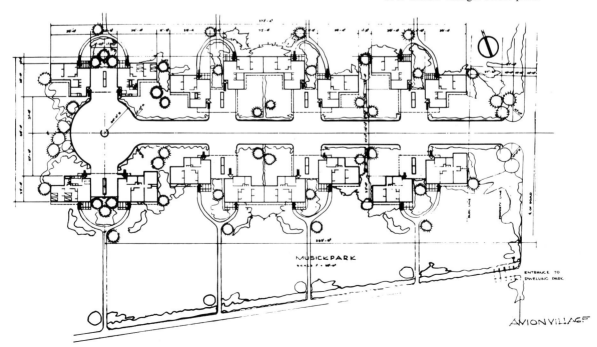

172. Elysian Park Heights, Los Angeles, 1953 (Project, Neutra and Alexander). Development seen from northwest.

173. Dusseldorf Theatre Competition, 1959.

174. Dusseldorf Theatre Competition. Auditorium interior.

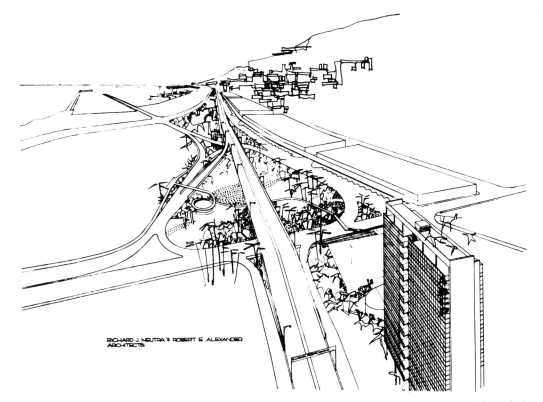

175. Redevelopment Plan for the Port of Carácas, Venezuela, 1955 (Project, Neutra and Alexander). Plaza at port entry.

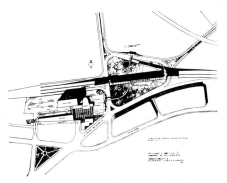

176. Carácas Redevelopment. Site plan.

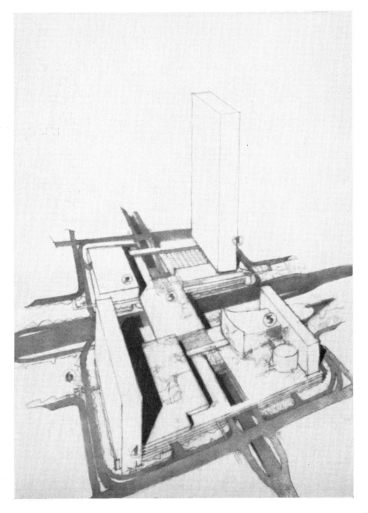

177. Carácas Redevelopment. Central nucleus of office tower, theatres, hotel, shopping center, and department store.

"Anatolian mosque"

"TRAVEL SKETCHES THROUGH LIFE"

During the spare moments when he travels, Richard Neutra sketches in a notepad. Whether sketching at the edge of a slow-winding creek in the high Transvaal veldt or recording the sights while waiting for an airport bus, Neutra shows his sympathetic awareness of . . ."the grand zoological garden to which we find admission through birth . . ."

"Adoration in curlicues"

"Parrot in a nunnery court, Latin America"

"Colorful chaos, Rio"

"Slavic dancers"

"Mothers and babies . . . in the Caribbean"

". . . and in Brazil"

"Band concert on the beach, Madras"

"Nuns and gauchos over the pampas"

"Bull ring seen from the shady side"

"Buddhists"

"Giraffe poorly fed,
    Africa"

SELECTED CHRONOLOGICAL LIST OF
BUILDINGS AND PROJECTS

1923   Competition for Business Center, Haifa. Eric Mendelsohn and Neutra. First prize. (Project)

1923–30   Rush City Reformed. (Project)

1927   Jardinette Apartments, Los Angeles.
Palace of League of Nations, Geneva. Neutra and R. M. Schindler. (Project)

1929   Lovell House (Health House), Los Angeles.

1933   Architect's Own House (V.D.L. Research House), Los Angeles.

1935   Beard House, Altadena. Awarded Gold Medal, Better Homes of America.
Corona Avenue School, Bell (Los Angeles). Honor Award, Pittsburgh Glass Competition.

1936   Plywood Model House, Los Angeles.
Von Sternberg House, Los Angeles.
California Military Academy, Los Angeles.

1937   Beckstrand House, Palos Verdes.

1938   Strathmore Apartments, West Los Angeles. Honor Award, Pittsburgh Glass Competition.
Emerson Junior High School, West Los Angeles.

1939   National Youth Administration Centers, Sacramento and San Luis Obispo.
Amity Village, Mutual Housing Development, Compton. (Project)

1941   Avion Village, Texas.

1942   Nesbitt House, West Los Angeles. AIA Honor Award.
Channel Heights, Federal Housing Development, San Pedro. Neutra and Dion Neutra. AIA Honor Award.
Kelton Apartments, West Los Angeles. AIA Honor Award.

1944	Rural schools and health centers, Puerto Rico. Urban schools, hospitals and health centers, Puerto Rico. (Project)

1944   Rural schools and health centers, Puerto Rico.
            Urban schools, hospitals and health centers, Puerto Rico. (Project)

1946   Kaufmann House (Desert House), Palm Springs. AIA Distinguished Honor Award.

1948   Tremaine House, Santa Barbara. AIA Citation.
            Aloe Medical Supply Building, Los Angeles. AIA Honor Award.
            Holiday House, Malibu. AIA Citation.
            Arts & Architecture Magazine Case Study House for Dr. Bailey. AIA Citation.

1950   Urban Redevelopment Plan for Sacramento.* *Progressive Architecture* Award. (Project)

1950–53   Elysian Park Heights, Urban Redevelopment for Los Angeles Housing Authority.* (Project)
            Eagle Rock Playground Club House, Los Angeles. AIA Citation.

1951   Hinds House, Los Angeles. AIA Honor Award.
            Northwestern Insurance Building, Los Angeles. AIA Honor Award.

1952   Moore House, Ojai. AIA Honor Award.

1953   Kester Avenue Elementary School, Los Angeles. AIA Honor Award.

1954   Child Guidance Clinic, Los Angeles.*
            Business Education Building, Orange Coast College, Costa Mesa.*

1955   San Bernardino Medical Center, San Bernardino.
            Science Building and Auditorium, St. John's College, Annapolis, Md.*

1956   Gemological Institute, West Los Angeles.

1957   Science Building, and Speech Arts and Music Auditorium, Orange Coast College, Costa Mesa.* AIA Citation.
            Miramar Chapel, La Jolla.*
            Alamitos Intermediate School, Garden Grove.*

1958   Riviera Methodist Church, Redondo Beach.*
            Elementary Training School, University of California at Los Angeles.*

1959   Düsseldorf Theater Competition, Germany. One of three winning awards. (Project)
            Dayton Museum of Natural History, Dayton, Ohio.*

1960   Singleton House, Los Angeles.

*Neutra and Alexander.

1960   *Work under construction:*

Lincoln Memorial Museum, Gettysburg, Pa.*
United States Embassy, Karachi, Pakistan.*
Hall of Records, Los Angeles.* In Association with Honnold and Rex;
James Friend; Herman C. Light & Associates.
Fine Arts Building, University of Nevada, Reno, Nevada.*
Richard J. Neutra School, Lemoore.*
Santa Ana Police Facilities Building, Santa Ana.*
Palos Verdes High School, Palos Verdes.*
Garden Grove Community Drive-In Church, Garden Grove.

*Neutra and Alexander. Associates: Architects Dion Neutra, Robert Pierce, and Howard
Miller; Engineers: Arthur Parker, Jack Zehnder and Boris
Lemos.
Collaborating on work in Neutra office: Benno Fischer, Serge Koschin and John Blanton.
Other collaborating architects: Thaddeus Longstreth, Princeton, N. J.;
Donald Haines Associates, San Francisco;
Yount, Sullivan and Lecklider, Ohio;
Ramberg and Lowrey, Santa Ana;
Carrington H. Lewis, Palos Verdes;
Lockhard, Casazza & Parsons, Reno, Nevada.

CHRONOLOGY

1892	Born in Vienna, Austria
1914–17	Served as artillery officer in Balkans
1917	Graduated from Technische Hochschule, Vienna
1922	Draftsman-collaborator, office of Eric Mendelsohn, Berlin Marriage to Dione Niedermann of Zürich
1923	Came to United States
1924	Office of Holabird and Roche, Chicago
1925	Office of Frank Lloyd Wright, Taliesin, Spring Green, Wisconsin
1926	Opened practice in Los Angeles
1928–29	Taught architecture, Academy of Modern Art, Los Angeles
1930	Delegate to Congrès International d'Architecture Moderne (CIAM) in Brussels Became United States citizen
1939–41	Member and chairman, California State Planning Board
1939	Consultant, U.S. Housing Authority
1941–42	Member, California Professional Standards Board
1942–43	Guest artist, Bennington College, Vermont
1944	Consultant and architect to Government of Puerto Rico
1947	Fellow, American Institute of Architects
1949	Partnership with Robert E. Alexander
1950	Honorary Doctor of Technical Sciences, University of Graz, Austria
1951	Consultant and architect to Civil Government of Guam
1954	Silver Medallion, Columbia University Honorary Doctor of Technical Sciences, Technical University of Berlin

1958   Gold Medal, Cuban Association of Architects
Honor Award, City of Vienna

1959   Order of Merit, Federal Republic of Germany
Honorary President, Sociedad de Arquitectos, Buenos Aires
Exner Medal, Austrian Gewerbeverein, Vienna

INDEX

Numbers in regular roman type refer to text pages; *italic* figures refer to the plates.

1973

THE PAINTING OF PICTURES

Respite, SEE COLORPLATE ON PAGE **131**